# Wild Animal Groups

**THIS EDITION**
**Editorial Management** by Oriel Square
**Produced for DK** by WonderLab Group LLC
Jennifer Emmett, Erica Green, Kate Hale, *Founders*

**Editors** Grace Hill Smith, Libby Romero, Maya Myers, Michaela Weglinski;
**Photography Editors** Kelley Miller, Annette Kiesow, Nicole di Mella; **Managing Editor** Rachel Houghton;
**Designers** Project Design Company; **Researcher** Michelle Harris; **Copy Editor** Lori Merritt;
**Indexer** Connie Binder; **Proofreader** Larry Shea; **Reading Specialist** Dr. Jennifer Albro;
**Curriculum Specialist** Elaine Larson

**Published in the United States by DK Publishing**
1745 Broadway, 20th Floor, New York, NY 10019

Copyright © 2023 Dorling Kindersley Limited
DK, a Division of Penguin Random House LLC
23 24 25 26 10 9 8 7 6 5 4 3 2 1
001–334119–Sept/2023

A catalog record for this book
is available from the Library of Congress.
HC ISBN: 978-0-7440-7550-2
PB ISBN: 978-0-7440-7552-6

DK books are available at special discounts when purchased in bulk for sales promotions, premiums,
fundraising, or educational use. For details, contact: DK Publishing Special Markets,
1745 Broadway, 20th Floor, New York, NY 10019
SpecialSales@dk.com

Printed and bound in China

The publisher would like to thank the following for their kind permission to reproduce their images:
a=above; c=center; b=below; l=left; r=right; t=top; b/g=background

**123RF.com:** Magdalena Paluchowska 6–7; **Alamy Stock Photo:** Sue Clark 12cla, John Digby 28cra, JHVEPhoto 23c, C.O. Mercial 24b,
Nature Picture Library / Doug Allan 20–21, Nature Picture Library / Konrad Wothe 25c, robertharding / Pablo Cersosimo 13bl,
Jonathan Steinbeck 27b; **Dreamstime.com:** Anankkml 1cb, Artushfoto 17tr, Patrice Correia 18b, Karoline Cullen 13crb,
Sarah Jane Duran 26t, Meg Forbes 27tr, Jan Havlicek 4–5, Isselee 3cb, 11br, Johncarnemolla 9b, Linncurrie 9tr, Owen Mather 6b,
Roman Murushkin 16–17, Win Nondakowit 14cl, Chinnasorn Pangcharoen 30b, Paulbroad 29c, Nikolay Petkov 28cl,
Sergey Uryadnikov 25tl; **Getty Images:** Frank Krahmer / Photographer's Choice RF 21cla, Stone / Tim Flach 14–15b;
**Getty Images / iStock:** Michel Viard 12tr, WLDavies 22–23; **Shutterstock.com:** Adalbert Dragon 10–11, click7 8, Aleksandr Kutskii 19t

Cover images: *Front:* **Dreamstime.com:** Picture.jacker; **Getty Images:** RooM / kristianbell b

All other images © Dorling Kindersley
For more information see: www.dkimages.com

## For the curious
**www.dk.com**

Level

3

# Wild Animal Groups

Libby Romero

# Contents

# Living Together

There are swarms of bees and packs of wolves. There are schools of fish in the ocean. There are towers of giraffes and flamboyances of flamingos. There are gaggles of geese and more.

Many animals live in groups all around the world. Living together helps them survive.

Animal groups vary in size. Some groups are small. Elephants live in family groups called herds. Once young males are able to take care of themselves, they leave the herd. They may live alone or join with a few other young bulls to form a small herd.

**So Many Birds**
With a population of about 1.5 billion, red-billed queleas are the most abundant wild bird species on Earth.

Other groups are huge. Flocks of red-billed queleas fly over the African savannah where elephants live. These fast-breeding birds sometimes swarm in flocks with millions of birds. It can take up to five hours for a massive flock to pass by.

# Finding Food

Living in a group has its advantages.
One benefit is finding food. Many animals
have evolved to hunt in groups.
A pride of lions is a familiar example.

Female lions are in charge of hunting. Usually, they go on the prowl at night. They work together to stalk, surround, and kill their prey. Whatever they catch is shared with all members of the pride.

**The Lunch Line**
When it's time to eat, the pride follows a specific order. Males go first, lionesses eat next, and cubs get the leftovers.

Orcas have developed creative ways to hunt together as a pack. Seals are some of their favorite prey. But seals tend to rest on ice floes, out of the orcas' reach. Orcas swim together and charge at the ice. They make a big wave that knocks seals into the water where they can nab them.

Fish are tasty, too, but one little fish isn't much of a meal. A pod of orcas herds a school of fish into a tight ball near the surface before they take a mouthful.

Orcas chase sea lions to shallow water. Then, they beach themselves on purpose to catch their prey when the sea lions flee to the shore.

Working together also helps orcas catch the most dangerous of meals. They have learned to flip rays and sharks upside down in the water. This temporarily paralyzes the rays and sharks. Without the stinger or teeth to deal with, orcas get an easy meal.

Even ants work together to find and gather food. Worker ants do all the work. As they search for food, they leave a trail of chemical scents called pheromones. When they find food, they double back. Other ants follow the trail to the food. Groups of ants take turns carrying chunks of food back to the nest.

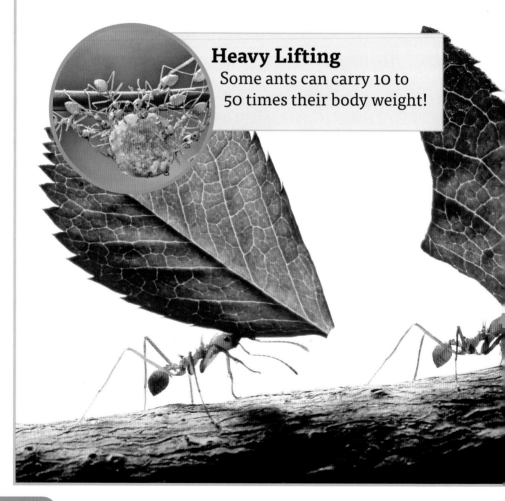

**Heavy Lifting**
Some ants can carry 10 to 50 times their body weight!

Leafcutter ants work together to grow their own food! Some worker ants bring pieces of leaves back to their underground nests. Others chew the leaves thoroughly. Then, gardener ants use the mush to grow a fungus they can eat. Some leafcutter ants even grow a bacterium that protects the colony's fungus garden from mold.

# Defending the Group

Being in a group also helps animals defend themselves. Sometimes, they must defend themselves against other animals.

One way to do that is to blend in. A dazzle of zebras is a dizzying mass of black and white stripes. It's hard for predators to single out individual zebras in the group.

## A Helping Hand

Ostriches and zebras often live together. Ostriches have great eyesight. Zebras have excellent hearing and a strong sense of smell. They warn each other about predators.

Another way animals defend themselves is by looking out for each other. Meerkat families live in groups called mobs. While some members of the mob forage for food, others stand at sharp attention. They scour the skies, searching for birds of prey. If they see one, they let out a sharp, shrill call. It's a warning to take cover—now!

Some animals are too big to take cover, and they have to protect their babies. If predators approach, the group fights back.

When wolves attack, musk oxen form a tight circle around their calves. Large bulls rush out of the circle and swipe at the wolves with their big, sharp horns. As long as the musk oxen stay in their circle, the calves are safe.

Sometimes, being in a group helps animals defend themselves against the environment. One of the best examples of this can be found at the bottom of the world—emperor penguins in Antarctica.

Emperor penguins don't build nests. Instead, the male penguin balances the egg on his feet under a layer of skin called a brood pouch. For about two months, he stands upright through the brutal Antarctic winter.

To keep warm, the father penguins huddle together in a large group. They take turns standing on the outside of the group so everyone has a chance to escape the icy cold.

**Different Penguin Groups**
A group of penguins walking on land is called a waddle. A group in the water is a raft. A large breeding group is a colony or rookery. And a group of chicks is a crèche.

# Coping with Change

Being in a group also helps animals cope with change. There are all sorts of changes in nature. Seasons are a prime example.

When seasons change, some animals follow heat. Monarch butterflies spend summers in Canada and the US. As winter approaches, one generation after another makes the long journey to warmer lands in Mexico and California, USA. The butterflies fly north again in the spring.

Other animals follow the rain. Rain makes plants grow, and plants mean food.

When the rainy season comes to Africa, the Great Migration begins. More than 1.5 million wildebeest begin their long annual trek in search of food and water.

Some changes happen quickly. When they do, animals in a group work together to solve the problem.

Chimpanzees have strong bonds in their troops. They help each other solve problems all the time. If one chimp has fleas, another kindly picks them off. If a mother chimpanzee dies, a different female will raise her young.

**Power Plays**
Male chimpanzees often fight to gain power. Females rely on relationships to keep their babies safe.

Chimpanzees even work together to help their friends or family members gain and stay in power. Having a close relationship with troop leaders boosts a chimp's own social standing. If the leader falls, they do, too.

Some changes happen over long periods of time. When those slow changes occur, animals are adapting. Parents pass new traits on to their offspring. Being in a group makes it easier to find a mate and pass on new traits more quickly.

As temperatures on Earth rise, scientists have noticed one change in some birds, like the red-rumped parrot and gang-gang cockatoo: their beaks have gotten bigger.

In the past 150 years, gang-gang cockatoo beaks have increased in size by as much as 10 percent. Why does this matter?
A bird can redirect heat to its beak, which keeps the rest of its body cooler. Evolving to have a bigger beak is one way to cope with climate change.

Living in a group means there are more mouths to feed. This makes it easier for diseases to pass from one animal to another. But for many animals, those disadvantages are minor compared to the benefits of group living. That's why so many animals live in groups.

The next time you see a cluster of spiders or a mischief of mice, stop, look, and think. How does living in a group help this kind of animal survive?

# Glossary

**Adapt**
To change in a way that makes a thing better suited to its environment

**Bacterium**
A tiny, one-celled living thing

**Beach**
To strand on the shore

**Evolve**
To change slowly over time in an attempt to ensure survival

**Forage**
To search for food or supplies

**Fungus**
A group of organisms that look like plants but cannot make their own food

**Huddle**
To gather in a small, close group

**Ice floe**
A piece of floating ice in the sea

**Offspring**
The child or young of a person, animal, or plant

**Paralyze**
To make unable to move

**Pheromone**
A chemical substance made by an animal to send signals or cause a reaction in another of the same species

**Predator**
An animal that eats other animals

**Prey**
An animal that is eaten by other animals

**Savannah**
A type of grassland with few trees

**Shrill**
Having a high, sharp sound

**Stalk**
To hunt in a slow, quiet manner

**Trait**
Characteristic passed down from one's parents

# Index

# Quiz

Answer the questions to see what you have learned. Check your answers in the key below.

1. What do worker ants use to guide other ants toward food?

2. What makes zebras blend with their group to help them avoid predators?

3. Why do male penguins huddle together in a large group?

4. What is the annual wildebeest trek in Africa called?

5. How does living in a group help parents pass on new traits more quickly?

1. A trail of pheromones  2. Stripes  3. To stay warm
4. The Great Migration  5. It makes it easier to find a mate